lonely planet

NOT-FOR-PARENTS

LONDON
Everything
you ever
wanted
to know

Klay Lampre

CONTENTS

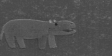

NOT-FOR-PARENTS

THIS IS NOT A GUIDEBOOK. And it is definitely Not-for-parents.

IT IS THE REAL, INSIDE STORY about
one of the world's most famous cities—London. In this book you'll hear
fascinating tales about famous and infamous people,
creepy underground places,
dark history and strange characters galore.

Check out cool stories about **graffiti artists**, murdered princes
and people from all over. You'll find royalty, **punks** and sleuths,
and some amazingly **weird food**.

This book shows you a **LONDON** your parents
probably don't even know about.

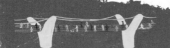

OLD FATHER THAMES

If only the Thames could talk. It has flowed through 2,000 years of invasions, fires, bombings, plague, and pollution, carrying its secrets of the great city to the North Sea. And without "Old Father Thames," it's doubtful that London would exist at all.

A moving story
What were lightermen and how were they different to watermen? Glad you asked. The lightermen moved stuff between ships and shore on barges called lighters. Watermen moved people from one side of the river to the other.

A FLOWING FREEWAY

Back when England had a huge empire, London was the busiest port in the world. These days, while large ships can still navigate the river all the way to London Bridge, you are more likely to see a party boat than a cargo ship.

High and dry
The Thames Barrier is a huge gate that stops London going under water when there are really high tides or storm surges coming up from the ocean.

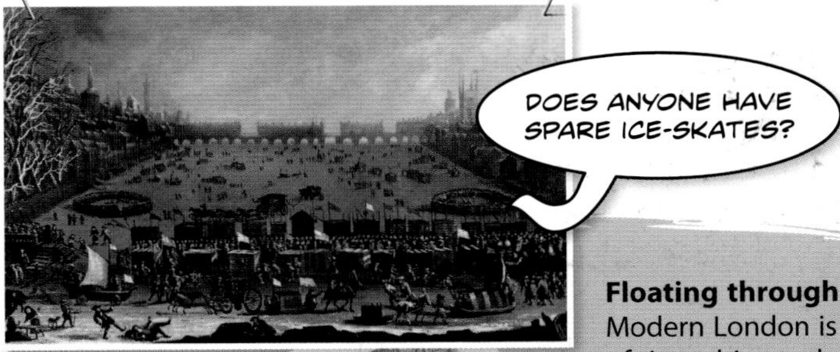
DOES ANYONE HAVE SPARE ICE-SKATES?

An icy reception
Hundreds of years ago when London winters were much colder, the Thames would often freeze over. Frost fairs were held on the ice, with shows, shops, and sports like ice-bowling.

Floating through centuries
Modern London is hundreds of times bigger than the little fortified port built by the Romans. But the Thames is still at the heart of the city.

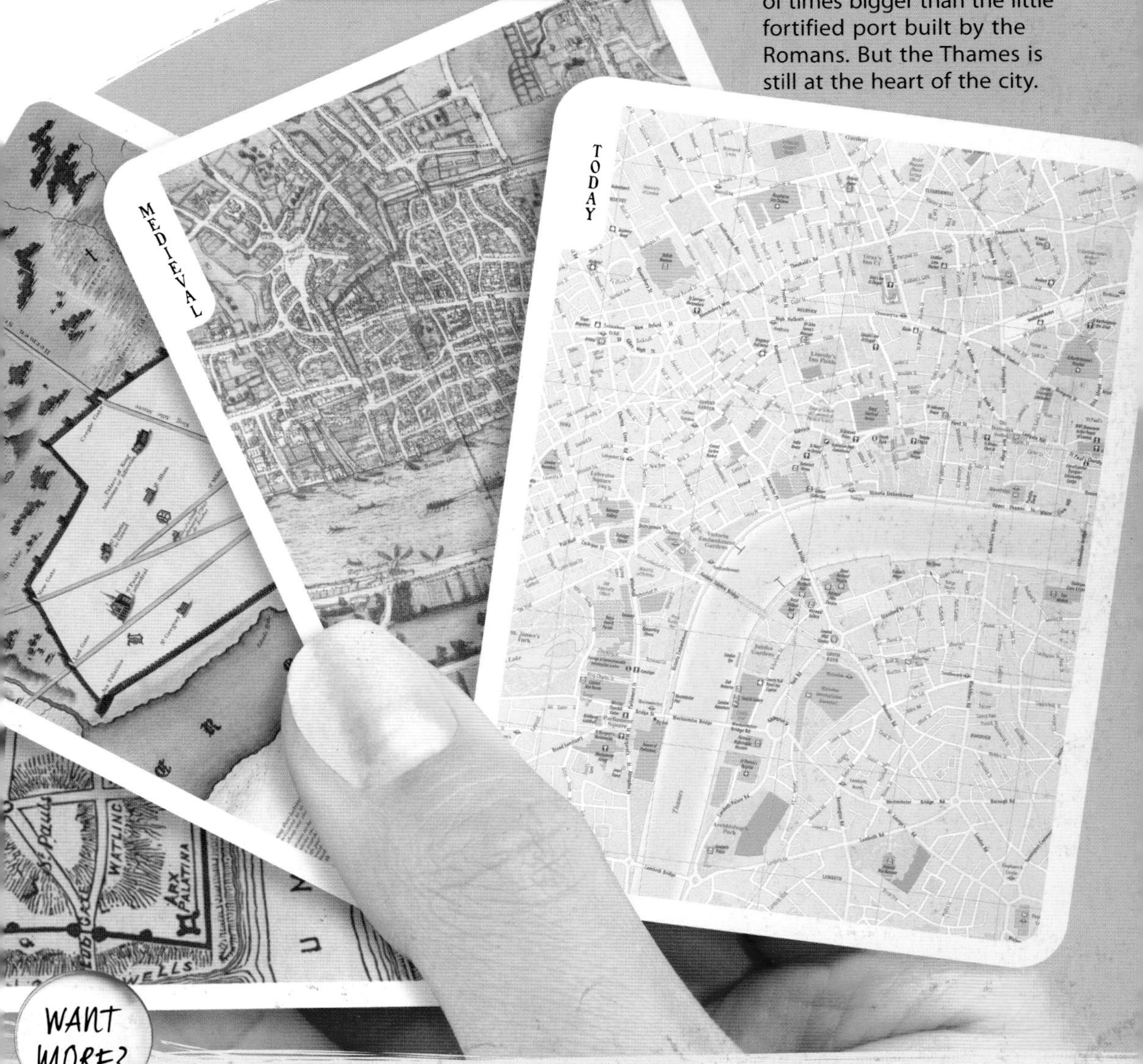
MEDIEVAL
TODAY
WATLING
ARX PALATINA

WANT MORE?

Museum of London—www.museumoflondon.org.uk

BELLY UP!

When you have no money to buy food, and no land to farm, what do you do? You catch some squirmy eels from the local river, boil them up, let them cool, and then eat them. If you can get past the slime factor, eels are good for you.

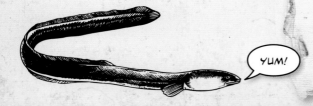

JELLIED EEL RECIPE

Ingredients (serves 4):
Two freshwater eels cleaned, gutted, and skinned, 1½ cups water, 5 tablespoons white wine vinegar, 10 black peppercorns, 1 bay leaf, salt, and a knob of butter.

Method:
Chop the eels into pieces about 2in (5cm) long.

Grease a casserole dish with the butter.

Put the eel pieces in the dish with the rest of the ingredients and season with the salt.

Put the lid on the casserole dish and bake in the oven at 325ºF (170ºC) for about an hour.

Let the eel and its liquor cool before putting it in the fridge overnight until the liquid has jellied.

Cut the slime
with spicy chili
vinegar.

Mash it up!
It's not a London meat pie and mashed potato without mushy peas or a green sauce that looks like it came from an alien's nose (but is really leftover eel juice mixed with parsley).

Bean there...
To start your day the London way, have some baked beans with your eggs, bacon, toast, and tea.

First fast food
Jellied eel is the original London fast food. Cockneys were the first to put jellied eel on the map. They caught the wriggling delicacy in the nearby Thames.

Frying times
Fish-and-chips is a longtime local favorite. In wartime, when other foods were hard to find or cost too much, Londoners could still get fish-and-chips from a "chippy."

The world on a plate
People moving to London from other parts of the world have introduced their own foods. Now there's nothing more London than eating a curry or kebab.

Eel coupons
In World War II food was limited and even eels were scarce. Shoppers were given coupons to use instead of money, so that everyone had a fair share of the food available.

WANT MORE?

The history of pie and mash—www.sweenytoddspieandmash.com/history

PASS THE ARMY AND NAVY

Cockneys are people from London's East End who have
a particular accent and use rhyming words as a way
of life. When they go up the stairs they use the "apples
and pears." When they take a "butcher's hook" they're
having a look. So if you're asked to pass the "army
and navy," of course you'd pass the gravy.

Behind the buttons
They call themselves the
Pearly Kings and Queens,
the people who raise money
for charity dressed in clothes
covered with pearl buttons.

Harvest hoot
The annual Harvest Festival is a
big day for Pearlies, riding like
royalty in donkey carts and
celebrating by dancing around
a maypole…you could get
dizzy watching them!

"Bumble refuses more porridge to the Workhouse boys."
(OLIVER TWIST)

A twist in the tale!

Nineteenth-century London was a tough place for poor people, and the author Charles Dickens wrote books about their problems. *Oliver Twist* is about an orphan who gets caught up with a gang of pickpockets.

COCKNEY RHYMING SLANG

1 CLOSE YOUR NORTH AND SOUTH.

2 HAVE YOU SEEN THE BAKED BEAN?

3 THIS IS MY TROUBLE AND STRIFE.

4 DON'T TELL ME A PORKY (PORK PIE).

5 HOP INTO MY JAM JAR.

6 MIND THOSE APPLES AND PEARS.

7 STOP, TEA LEAF!

8 LET'S GET DOWN TO BRASS TACKS.

9 I THINK HE'S BROWN BREAD.

10 I'M GOING TO HIT THE FROG AND TOAD.

Answers: 1. Mouth; 2. Queen; 3. Wife; 4. Lie; 5. Car; 6. Stairs; 7. Thief; 8. Facts; 9. Dead; 10. Road

Fair enough

In *Pygmalion* written by George Bernard Shaw, a professor teaches a Cockney flower-girl to act and speak like a "lady." In *My Fair Lady*, which is the movie version, actress Audrey Hepburn (right) has to fake a Cockney accent.

Give us a ring

Only Londoners born within hearing distance of the church bells of St. Mary-le-Bow are said to be true Cockneys. Careful! If you pretend to be a Cockney because you think it's cool, you'll get called a "Mockney."

WANT MORE?

I SPY THE LONDON EYE

So can most of London! The London Eye is a massive wheel that gives passengers a view of the whole of the city and beyond. At its highest point it is 443ft (135m) above ground—as high in the sky as 26 giraffes standing on one another's heads. You could say it's wheely wheely big!

I CAN SEE THE ZOO FROM HERE.

OW, MY NECK!

Hard to top
On a clear day you can see for 25 miles (40km) from the highest point of the London Eye—all the way to Windsor Castle!

HOW IT WORKS

With a central hub connected to outer and inner rims by cable spokes, it spins kind of like a big bicycle wheel! Each rotation takes about a half hour, so the Eye goes slow enough for people to get on and off without the wheel having to stop.

Behind the wheel

It took seven years to build the Eye, and then a week to lift it up. They used the same technology that helps build deep-water oil rigs. The Eye is kept in place with many piles and cables, which are held down by 3,750 tons (3,400t) of concrete.

WHY DO I FEEL LIKE I'VE BEEN HERE BEFORE?

32 capsules

64 spoke cables

A-frame

Concrete foundations

Take a ride

The passenger capsules don't hang under the wheel like in a regular Ferris wheel. They turn within rings attached to the main rim, so there's a completely unblocked view from the top of the Eye.

Eye say! You're late!

The Eye was supposed to open to the public by New Year's Day 2000, but it missed the date. A technical problem meant the capsules could have turned upside down as the wheel turned! The wheel finally opened in March 2000.

WANT MORE?

The London Eye official website—www.londoneye.com

ONE DOES SO ENJOY BEING ROYAL

Being royal means being a king or queen, or being closely related to one. It's a big deal. You get a special title, a big house, and money from the government. The trick is becoming royal. There are only two ways you can do that—be born a royal or marry a royal.

1100
1200
1300
1400
1500

Norman
Plantagenet
Lancaster → York → Tudo

🦐 Norman 1066–1154
🦐 Plantagenet 1154–1399
🦐 Lancaster 1399–1471
🦐 York 1471–1485
🦐 Tudor 1485–1603
🦐 Stuart 1603–1714
Hanover 1714–1901
Windsor 1901–now

Ruling back the years
The families that have ruled England, from William the Conqueror in the 11th century to current-day Queen Elizabeth II, have had their fair share of fights and battles for power.

WE CAME OVER FROM FRANCE

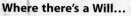

Better Ed than dead
Edward III was a popular king who ruled for 50 years in the 14th century. He was victorious in many battles but was helpless against the bubonic plague, which killed one third of England's population.

WE HAD SIX WIVES

Where there's a Will...
The first Norman king of England, William I, earned his nickname "William the Conqueror" by defeating the last Anglo-Saxon king of England. Before then he was called "William the Bastard."

WE LOVE A BIT OF WARMONGERING

Heartless Henry
One of England's most colorful kings, Henry VIII created the Church of England and waged many wars, but he is best known for marrying six women— and killing two of them!

The Windsor family's original name of Saxe-Coburg-Gotha is German!

WE WENT MAD!

By George!
George III had a mixed reign. He lost Britain's American colonies but helped England become a European power. Unfortunately, he went mad so his son had to take over.

1600 1700 1800 1900 2000

Stuart   Hanover   Windsor

Queen of hearts
Elizabeth I, daughter of Henry VIII, overcame a bad childhood (Daddy had Mummy's head chopped off) and became a great and popular queen, ruling over England's "Golden Age."

WE OWNED 3,000 DRESSES!

Edward VIII
Edward became king after the death of his father George, but he gave the gig away. Why? Being king meant he couldn't marry his girlfriend because royalty could not marry people who had been divorced.

I GOT RID OF 'EM FOR 11 YEARS

A RIGHT ROYAL PAIN
Originally a soldier, Oliver Cromwell was a king's worst nightmare. He had Charles I executed, forced Charles II into exile, and then became Britain's "Lord Protector." He ended wars against Portugal and Holland, and defeated Spain. But then he died and the royals were soon back in charge.

WE GAVE IT UP TO MARRY THE WOMAN WE LOVED.

WANT MORE?

IT'S ABOUT TIME

If you didn't have a watch or a cell phone—or a computer or a microwave or a radio or the television—how would you tell the time? You'd need a big clock you could see from a distance, something that tick-tocked every minute and made a fuss every hour, like London's Big Ben. This big clock tower has been London's timekeeper for more than 150 years.

WE DON'T HAVE TIME TO HANG AROUND!

CLEAN YOUR CLOCK

To keep Big Ben looking good, a team of cleaners has to abseil down ropes to reach the four dials of the clock. They make sure to keep out of strong winds so they don't

C'MON BIG BOY, GIVE US A TINKLE.

Running repairs

The company that looks after Big Ben has staff on call at all times to fix the clock if needed. Workers wind up the clock three times a week to keep it ticking along.

BIG BEN = 13.2 TONS

Just a bell

Big Ben is really just the bell in the Palace of Westminster clock tower, not the whole tower.

Third time lucky

The original hands were too heavy for the clock to work properly so they had to be remade. But even this didn't do the job so they had to make the hands again, and again.

Heavy snow once caused Big Ben to ring in the New Year 10 minutes late.

I NEED A NEW JOB. THESE HOURS ARE KILLING ME!

TIME FOR MORE

Big Ben may be the king of London's clocks, but there are other interesting timepieces throughout the city—both big and small.

Time in the sun

This golden old sundial is on the tower of St. Clement Danes church.

Shop clock

The Fortnum & Mason clock is on the front of a fancy food shop. Every hour, a mini Mr. Fortnum and Mr. Mason come out and bow to each other.

WANT MORE?

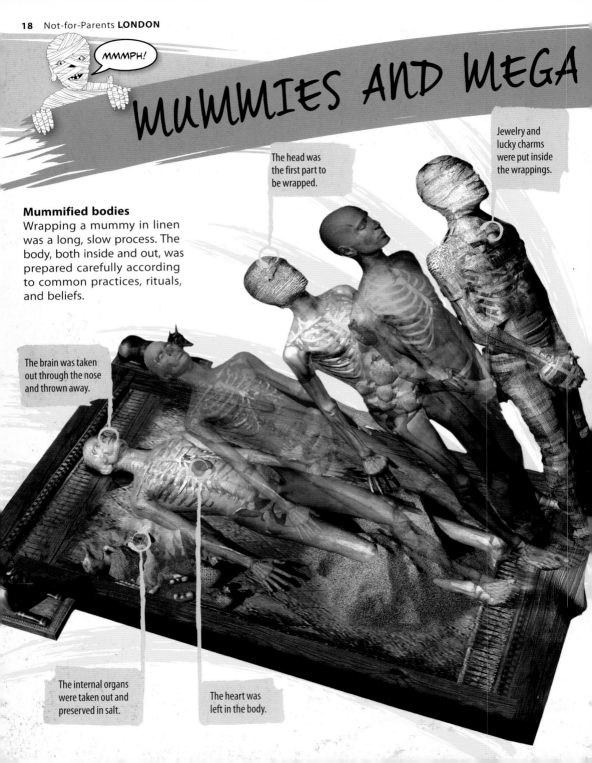

MMMPH!

MUMMIES AND MEGA

Mummified bodies

Wrapping a mummy in linen was a long, slow process. The body, both inside and out, was prepared carefully according to common practices, rituals, and beliefs.

The head was the first part to be wrapped.

Jewelry and lucky charms were put inside the wrappings.

The brain was taken out through the nose and thrown away.

The internal organs were taken out and preserved in salt.

The heart was left in the body.

TREASURES

In Ancient Egypt, when someone died their body was embalmed and then wrapped in linen cloths to preserve it... yuuuucckkk! The British Museum holds some of the most famous treasures in the world, and many visitors start with the creepy mummies.

GET ME OUT OF HERE...

ME TOO!

Mummies and pets
There are more mummies in this museum than anywhere outside Egypt. There are even mummies of cats, apes, and an eel.

Ancient cylindrical socket

Gold chariot model

TREASURES GALORE

Many amazing, ancient objects have been saved and gathered for display in the British Museum. Some are even thousands of years old, which means they were made centuries before there were any "modern" tools.

Roman vase

WANT MORE?

The British Museum—www.britishmuseum.org

HARRY POTTER ON LOCATION

Even Muggles can see the locations in London that were used in the *Harry Potter* film series. These include the spot at London Zoo where Harry discovers he can talk to snakes, as well as the marble floors and chandeliers of Gringotts Bank. This is really the Exhibition Hall of Australia House, where there are no goblins to be seen…we think!

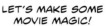

LET'S MAKE SOME MOVIE MAGIC!

1 Platform 9¾
This is the arched wall between platforms nine and ten at King's Cross Station. Anyone who tries to jump through this wall is in for a trip to the doctor!

❶ Kings Cross
❷ London Zoo
❸ Westminster
❹ Leadenhall Market

THEY TOLD ME I WAS GOING TO BE A SSSSSSSSSTAR.

THESE ACTORS REALLY CAST A SPELL ON THE AUDIENCE!

2 Speaking Parseltongue
London Zoo's reptile house is where Harry speaks to his first snake, a Burmese python—but the snake that really lives there is a black mamba.

4 Leadenhall Market

This 130-year-old Victorian market is not only where some *Harry Potter* scenes were filmed, it is also where Lara Croft rode her motorbike in *Tomb Raider*!

I JUST LOVE CAUSING A STIR!

Leaky Cauldron

A shopfront in a tight passage of Leadenhall Market became the entrance to "The Leaky Cauldron" in *Harry Potter and the Goblet of Fire*.

ALL ABOARD!

People from all over the world head to "Platform 9¾" at King's Cross Station hoping that—just maybe—they'll be able to catch the famous Hogwarts Express to the School of Witchcraft and Wizardry (the train was actually filmed in the Scottish Highlands).

3 Westminster

Westminster underground station became the Ministry of Magic. Locals were grumpy when the station was closed for filming and they couldn't catch their trains.

WANT MORE?

JOURNEY TO THE CENTER

THEY TREAT US
LIKE ANIMALS
DOWN HERE!

SOMEHOW I'VE GOT TO
ESCAPE THE RAT RACE

Way down deep below the streets of London millions of people are traveling through dark tunnels, using the underground train system called the Tube. It may not be quite the center of the Earth, but it can feel like it as you head down more than 200ft (60m) below the surface.

Tube tails
You find more than people in the Underground. Rats and mice love the darkness, and hawks are sometimes used to stop pigeons building their nests in the tunnels.

OF THE EARTH

Crowded carriages
The London Underground carries more than three million passengers a day. Sometimes it gets so busy that stations have to be shut for safety.

Ghost trains
When they were excavating the Underground, many lines had to go through pits where plague victims were buried. Some people believe this disturbed spirits that now haunt the tunnels.

BOO!

Hole lot of hard work
The earliest tunnels were cut into the ground then covered up. Later, the use of tunneling shields kept it all below ground.

UNDERGROUND

Signs on the lines
The Tube system's famous round logos are known as roundels, bull's-eyes, or targets. Each Tube station has its own roundel displaying its name in the central bar.

I REALLY DIG MY WORK!

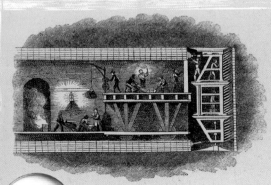

TUNNEL VISION

The Brunel tunnel that runs under the River Thames was built between 1825 and 1843 by French engineer Marc Brunel and his son. It was the first tunnel to be dug under a river, which is why people called it the eighth wonder of the world. Later it became part of the East London Underground line.

WANT MORE?

London Transport Museum—www.ltmuseum.co.uk

JURASSIC CLASSICS

Most people didn't know about dinosaurs until 1853 when some Englishmen made them famous. Sculptor Benjamin Waterhouse Hawkins worked with zoologist Richard Owen to create life-size models of the prehistoric beasts. To launch their education campaign, they invited a group of famous scientists to have dinner inside an Iguanodon!

DOING MORE FOR THE DINOSAUR

WOW!

Owen not only made the world aware of this important group of extinct creatures, but he also invented the word "dinosaur!" Inside the Natural History Museum, which he helped develop, scientists study new dinosaur finds. The main hall is dominated by Dippy the Dino—a cast of a Diplodocus skeleton.

On with the show
In 1853 the dinosaur models featured in the gardens of the Crystal Palace, part of a grand exhibition showcasing British industrial skill. They were prepared in the Extinct Animals room (left).

Extinct but everlasting
After its time in Hyde Park, the Crystal Palace building was moved to Sydenham Park south of London. The Crystal Palace burned down but Hawkins's and Owen's dinosaurs are still there!

I'M A MOA. THIS IS MY MATE RICHARD OWEN.

WANT MORE?

The Natural History Museum—www.nhm.ac.uk

ART OR MESS?

There's a lot of graffiti in London, but some of it has become famous. About 20 years ago graffiti started to appear on walls and trains in Bristol. The artist was a mysterious man called Banksy. Now graffiti is found in London and all over the world.

I'VE BEEN FISHING FOR YEARS AND ALL I'VE CAUGHT IS THIS LETTUCE LEAF.

"I USE WHATEVER IT TAKES. SOMETIMES THAT JUST MEANS DRAWING A MUSTACHE ON A GIRL'S FACE ON SOME BILLBOARD."

BANKSY, Mystery Artist

From street to shop
Banksy is now so popular that his graffiti is often saved by councils instead of being cleaned up. Now a Banksy shop has opened.

Don't try this at home
Banksy's artworks are made quite
simply with cardboard stencils and
cans of spray paint.

Spot the rat
Many of Banksy's works feature
a rat—it's his trademark animal.

Guess who
Only a few people in the world know
who Banksy is. He won't tell anyone his
name. Some people have described him
as "tall and skinny," others as "short and fat."

WANT
MORE?

The official Banksy website—www.banksy.co.uk

NOT ANOTHER ST. PAUL'S!

This cathedral should really be called St. Paul's No. 5. Since the year 604, five different St. Paul's have been built on the same site, which is the highest point in the City of London. The current building is over 300 years old, and it was the tallest building in the city up until 50 years ago.

Old St. Paul's
The cathedral that stands today replaced a St. Paul's (right) that was destroyed in the Great Fire of 1666 when most of London burned to the ground (see pages 52–53).

I'M A VIKING WITH A LIKING FOR STRIKING!!!

NOW THAT'S WHAT I CALL A CHURCH!

Careful with that match!
The Saxons built the first St. Paul's in 604. It burned down after about 70 years so they replaced it. This St. Paul's was burned down by marauding Vikings in 962. The third St. Paul's also burned down. And the fourth. No wonder the fifth St. Paul's is made of stone!

1

2

Three domes in one

3

Top stuff

The dome of St. Paul's is actually three domes in one. There's an inner dome, a brick cone that supports the tower on top, and an outer "skin." Together they weigh about as much as 13,000 fully grown elephants!

YOU'RE TALKING IN CIRCLES AGAIN!

CIRCLE OF SOUND

A narrow stairway with over 250 steps leads to the cathedral's Whispering Gallery, which runs round the inside of the dome. People on opposite sides of the gallery can whisper into the walls and hear each other clearly!

WANT MORE?

The architect was Sir Christopher Wren ✭ **St. Paul's Cathedral—www.stpauls.co.uk**

MEET THE WINDSORS

Queen Elizabeth II has four children and eight grandchildren. They are royals by birth, and though they usually only use their first name, their surname is Windsor. There are also royals by marriage. They can keep their own surname or become Windsor. But just to complicate the name game, not everyone gets a royal title...

I HOPE THIS BALCONY HOLDS...

Smile and wave
The balcony on the east face of Buckingham Palace is where the Windsors and their extended family gather to say hello to large crowds of royal subjects and tourists.

CROWNING DAY

The ceremony in which a prince or princess is crowned king or queen is called a coronation. Over the last 900 years, the coronation of every English king or queen has taken place in London's Westminster Abbey. Queen Elizabeth was crowned on June 2, 1953. She was 27.

Where the bucks stop
British taxpayers foot the bill for the Queen's staff, travel, palace upkeep, and personal expenses. In turn she and her family do plenty of work for charity around the world and give back any money made from royal property. Fair deal?

Before "Windsor" the British royals didn't have a surname.

**Her Majesty
Queen Elizabeth II
b. Apr 21, 1926**

Married
Nov 20, 1947

**Prince Phillip
Duke of Edinburgh
b. Jun 10, 1921**

**Prince Charles
Prince of Wales
b. Nov 14, 1948**

Married Jul 29, 1981
Divorced Aug 28, 1996

Married
Apr 9, 2005

**Princess Anne
b. Aug 15, 1950**

Married Nov 14, 1973
Divorced Apr 28, 1992

Married
Dec 12, 1992

**Prince Andrew
Duke of York
b. Feb 19, 1960**

Married Jul 23, 1986
Divorced May 30, 1996

**Prince Edward
Earl of Wessex
b. Mar 10, 1964**

Married Jul 19, 1999

**Diana Spencer
Princess of Wales
b. Jul 1, 1961
d. Aug 31, 1997**

**Mark Phillips
b. Sep 22, 1948**

**Sarah Ferguson
Duchess of York
b. Oct 15, 1959**

**Sophie Rhys-Jones
Countess of Wessex
b. Jan 20, 1965**

**Camilla Parker Bowles
Duchess of Cornwall
b. Jul 17, 1947**

**Timothy Laurence
b. Mar 1, 1955**

**Prince William
b. June 21, 1982**

**Prince Harry
b. Sep 15, 1984**

**Peter Phillips
b. Nov 15, 1977**

**Zara Phillips
b. May 15, 1981**

**Princess Beatrice
b. Aug 8, 1988**

**Princess Eugenie
b. Mar 23, 1990**

**Lady Louise
b. Nov 8, 2003**

**Viscount Severn
b. Dec 17, 2007**

New family member
On April 29, 2011, Prince William married Kate Middleton. The couple will be known as the Duke and Duchess of Cambridge.

Royal sexism?
When a royal marries a commoner—someone who isn't royal—only the brides become a princess or queen. If you're a man marrying a royal, you and your children can forget about titles.

WANT MORE?

SHOCK CHIC!

A few years back the world was shocked when teenagers started wearing ripped clothes, putting rings through their eyebrows and noses, dyeing their hair bright pink, and smashing into each other as they listened to loud songs about bad behavior. They were called punks, and they were outrageous. Now you wouldn't blink if you saw a punk on the street!

Dyed hair

Oi!

Studded collar

Metal chain

Leather jacket

Loud T-shirt

Tight pants

Chunky boots

Changing times
London's original punk scene began more than 30 years ago as a kind of anti-fashion movement. Today, there are punk-influenced clothing stores all over the city!

Pick your punk
This girl is a pretty standard punk, but there are many types—from the original Street and Glam punks, to more modern Skate and Pop varieties.

I USED TO BE CUTTING EDGE!

Shooting stars

They only lasted for a couple of years, but London band the Sex Pistols kicked off the city's punk era. Their lead singer was rotten and their bass player was vicious: Johnny Rotten and Sid Vicious.

The Sex Pistols song "God Save the Queen" caused outrage in the UK!

Looking sharp

Hair can be spiked up to the max with sugar and water, soap, gel, hair spray, or even glue!

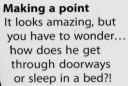

Making a point

It looks amazing, but you have to wonder… how does he get through doorways or sleep in a bed?!

Brush with care!

A punk favorite is a big strip of hair across the top of the head like some Native Americans used to wear. It is called a mohawk or mohican.

Close shaves

Skinheads are pretty punky, and while they wear all kinds of clothes, tattoos, and accessories, you can always pick one—they have no hair!

WHY DO THEY CALL ME EGGHEAD?!

Fringe benefits

Shave a bit, spike a bit, leave a bit—that's the way to create what's called a feathercut or Chelsea mohawk.

WANT MORE?

Punk fans danced "The Pogo" ☆ **Punk rock in the UK—www.punk77.co.uk**

MIX AND MINGLE

In 1948 the boat *Empire Windrush* brought a group of immigrants from the Caribbean to London. Many of the passengers were young men who had served in the military for Britain during World War II, returning to help rebuild Britain after the war and make a good life for their families. The media was in a frenzy and Parliament in hot debate about whether this was a boatload of "blacks" taking British jobs.

Journey to a new home
The *Empire Windrush* was the first of many ships to bring West Indian migrants to England. It sailed from Kingston, Jamaica and arrived in London on June 22, 1948.

Life of the *Empire Windrush*
Empire Windrush in her former life was a German cruise ship called *Monte Rosa*, used by the Nazi party. In the war she became a transport ship before being captured by the British. She sank in 1954.

CELEBRATING LIFE

Carnival in the Caribbean is a way of life. Colorful costumes with hectic headdresses, mad music, and wild dancing express the joy of life. Every year the massive Notting Hill Carnival celebrates the joy of life that Caribbean culture has brought to London.

RED, BLACK, GREEN, AND GOLD ARE MY COLORS!

The look of devotion
Rastafari is a modern religion practiced mainly in Jamaica, Africa, and England. For Rastas the body is the temple of God, which is why Rastas don't cut their hair, and often have dreadlocks.

THEY COME TO SEE ME PLAY BUT WON'T LET ME INTO HOTELS!

TRIUMPH OF SPIRIT

Learie Constantine was one of England's finest cricketers and most famous immigrants from the Caribbean. Though he was admired for his skill in sport, he suffered hurtful prejudice that inspired him to become a political activist, journalist, and lawyer. For his efforts he was knighted and made a baron.

Sounds and scents
Around a million people take part in the annual Notting Hill Carnival. Live bands and DJs roll out the sounds of calypso, samba, and soca while the smell of traditional Caribbean fare from food stalls fills the air.

WANT MORE?

The Notting Hill Carnival official site—www.thenottinghillcarnival.com

WHO'S THE MAN?

Long before *CSI*, *Dexter*, *Law and Order*, and *The Mentalist* there was Sherlock Holmes. He was the ultimate detective, using his wits to outsmart criminals and solve the crime before the police every time. Holmes was created by the Scottish writer Sir Arthur Conan Doyle.

Sir Arthur Conan Doyle, author

WATSON, I SEEM TO BE QUITE STUCK.

Tall tribute
The statue outside Baker Street tube station presents Holmes as we've come to know him, in a cape and deerstalker hat with a calabash pipe in hand. To trick suspects he often wore disguises.

SIR ARTHUR CONAN DOYLE
THE SIGN OF FOUR

THE ADVENTURES OF SHERLOCK HOLMES
A. CONAN DOYLE

Look for the clues...
Passengers on the London Underground can't miss this clue to the home address of the famous detective. His pipe-smoking silhouette is painted on the tiled walls of Baker Street Station.

ELEMENTARY, MY DEAR WATSON.

The secret of his success

Holmes was big on detail and fast on logic. A spot of mud on a shoe might be all he'd need to work out when the crime took place and where the criminal could be found.

CLUED IN?

1 WHO CREATED SHERLOCK HOLMES?

2 WHY WAS HIS LANDLADY FRUSTRATED?

3 WHAT PIPE DID HOLMES SMOKE?

4 WHAT WAS WATSON'S PROFESSIONAL TITLE?

5 HOW DID HOLMES SOLVE CRIMES?

Answers: 1. Sir Arthur Conan Doyle; 2. Holmes was messy, played loud music, and carried out smelly experiments; 3. Calabash; 4. Doctor; 5. Detail and logic.

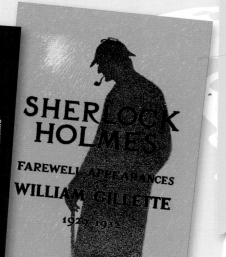

Holmes and Watson

Holmes's good friend, Dr. Watson, is his assistant and also the narrator of most of the stories. It is from Watson we learn of the brilliant detective's heavy duty ego and odd habits...

HOLMES'S HOME & MUSEUM

At the time the stories were being written, house numbers in Baker Street only went up to 100. Recently, the Sherlock Holmes Museum was given permission to use the address of 221b Baker Street, which was where Holmes lived. He rented rooms from Mrs. Hudson, who was forever frustrated by his mess, his loud music, and his smelly scientific experiments.

WANT MORE?

The Sherlock Holmes Museum—www.sherlock-holmes.co.uk/home.htm

NOTHING SQUARE IN TRAFALGAR

Busy Trafalgar Square is where people arrange
to meet for a cup of tea or a massive protest.
It's also home to Lord Nelson, four lions, and
loads of pigeons.

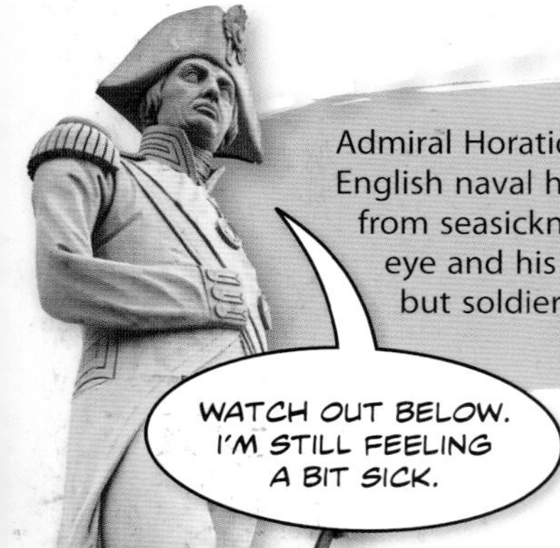

Admiral Horatio Nelson was a brave
English naval hero, who suffered
from seasickness! He lost his right
eye and his right arm in battle
but soldiered on.

WATCH OUT BELOW.
I'M STILL FEELING
A BIT SICK.

When Nelson died at the
Battle of Trafalgar, his body
was pickled in brandy.

THE NEXT KID
THAT CLIMBS ON
ME WILL GET A
BITE ON THE BUTT.

Legend says that if
Big Ben chimes
thirteen times the
four bronze lions
around Nelson's
Column will wake up.

Careful with those crumbs! Feeding the pigeons can get you fined £500.

There were once as many as 35,000 pigeons flapping around the Square. All the poo they produced was a prized fertilizer, and guards were paid to stop thieves stealing it.

WHO ARE YOU CALLING FAT?

Nelson's Column is 185ft (56m) high. It may not look that high, but try pacing 56 long strides and you will get an idea.

This statue of King George IV is rather flattering. In real life the king was very fat—so fat that his nickname was the Prince of WHALES.

WANT MORE?

Lord,

THE GREAT PLAGUE

1665. The year of the Great Plague. The disease is also called the Black Death because of the dark lumps that appear on the skin of victims. The rich leave the city. The poor have no option but to stay. Over 1,000 people are dying each week. They have no idea how it started or how it spreads, so the authorities decree that victims and their families should be shut into their houses and left to die.

Varieties of plague
Humans are affected by three kinds of plague: bubonic, septicaemic, and pneumonic. They cause internal bleeding, which results in black bruises, and they are all lethal.

Good for business
Some people made good money out of the plague. "Magic" potions and religious trinkets sold well. People were paid to uncover and report new cases, to cart bodies, and to clean houses after deaths.

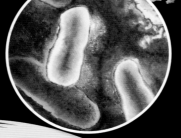

THEY ALSO KILLED 40,000 DOGS AND 80,000 CATS!

FLEAS AT FAULT

Rats are often blamed for the plague and they are guilty, but only by association. It was actually the fleas on the rats that carried the disease. Killing rats and other animals that might be diseased made the problem worse—the fleas jumped onto humans. This was only discovered around 200 years after the plague.

Sick sense
In addition to constant tolling of the death bells, Londoners endured the terrible smell of sickness. People burned strong incense and carried bundles of dried flowers and herbs to sniff.

↑ *Triumphant Death chases Londoners from their city 1665–66*

Medical mask
Most real doctors left London. Those who stayed wore a beaked mask full of herbs to cover the smell and protect themselves in case disease spread in air.

IT'S NOT A LOOK I GENERALLY GO IN FOR...

WANT MORE?

The Great Plague—www.inlondonguide.co.uk/london-history/the-great-plague

MEMORY LANE

1670–1710
Huguenots

Charles II offered sanctuary to Protestant people who were being persecuted in Catholic France. About half of the Huguenots that moved to England settled in London and worked as silk weavers.

1881–1914
Orthodox Jews

Many Jewish people fled Eastern Europe in the late 19th century, with about 150,000 of them settling in London. Among the first were actors from Russia who opened a theater just off Brick Lane.

1947–now
Bengalis

Today almost 70% of the people who live in the area surrounding Brick Lane can trace their origins to Bangladesh. It's the best place in London to shop for a curry—or a sari.

It remembers centuries ago when the French moved in, escaping violence in their country. It remembers a few decades ago when it was called "little Jerusalem" and shop signs were written in Yiddish. And it will always remember the smells from the curry houses of the Bengalis who now call it home.

THIS IS MAKING ME HUNGRY!

Spice it up!
The Brick Lane Curry Festival has been held every year since 1998, with more than 50 restaurants and 200 chefs now taking part in the event.

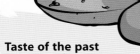

Taste of the past
Few of Brick Lane's Jewish residents remain, but there are still some shops on Brick Lane that sell tasty bagels with smoked salmon and cream cheese.

Cheers!
Huguenot immigrants taught the English better ways of making beer and helped make the Truman Brewery on Brick Lane the biggest beer factory in London.

Second-hand Sundays
Brick Lane's curry houses get busy on weekends when street performers and second-hand stalls draw large crowds.

WANT MORE?

Brick Lane official website—www.visitbricklane.org

CREEP ME OUT!

The bodies of some of the most famous people of all time are buried in the church of Westminster Abbey. Some are in stone vaults with a statue of themselves on top, others are stowed away in tombs along the walls, and there are loads right under the floor where you walk.

Ghostly Abbey
Some people claim that ghosts wander the Abbey at night. John Bradshaw, who signed the death warrant of Charles I, has supposedly been spotted wandering about, as has a monk who was murdered.

Slabs for scientists
Sir Isaac Newton explained gravity and the way that planets revolve around the Sun. Charles Darwin caused a fuss by suggesting natural selection, not God, created living things.

NOW WHY DIDN'T THIS APPLE FALL UP?

Sir Isaac Newton

Charles Dickens

Charles Darwin

CHARLES DICKENS
BORN 7TH FEBRUARY 1812
DIED 9TH JUNE 1870

Rudyard Kipling

Poets' Corner
Famous writers are buried in a section of the Abbey called Poets' Corner. Rudyard Kipling wrote the famous *Jungle Book*. Charles Dickens wrote about the hard life of the poor in England in books like *Oliver Twist*.

CROWNING ACHIEVEMENT

Every King or Queen of England and Britain since 1066 has been crowned at the Abbey. The same oak coronation throne has been used since 1308.

Kings and queens, poets and priests

In the church and cloisters of the Abbey, around 3,000 people are buried. There are also more than 600 monuments and memorials.

Queen of Scots, in a box

Mary Queen of Scots had a tough start in life and things didn't end so well either. She was put in prison for 19 years and then beheaded.

Mary Queen of Scots

Wife #4 is under the floor

Anne of Cleves was Henry VIII's fourth wife. He didn't meet her before the wedding then called the marriage quits after six months because he said Anne wasn't attractive!

Anne of Cleves

UNKNOWN SOLIDER

At the west end of the Abbey lies the body of a British soldier brought back from war in France. His tomb is a tribute to all who are sent to fight and die in wars, especially those with no known grave.

WANT MORE?

Westminster Abbey—www.westminster-abbey.org

Printing money
A collection of Shakespeare's plays published in 1623 sold recently for almost six million dollars. That makes it one of the world's most expensive books.

MR. POPULAR

The poet and playwright William Shakespeare was loved when he was alive and he's still a big deal today. Shakespeare is often called the greatest writer in the English language. So how did he keep his name at the top of the popularity polls for over 400 years? Maybe it's because so much of what he wrote are things we now say every day.

Globe theater

The Globe was "open air," with a narrow thatched roof around the edges. It was built from timber, including some very heavy beams.

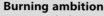

I can see my house from up here!

Are these the stairs to marriage?

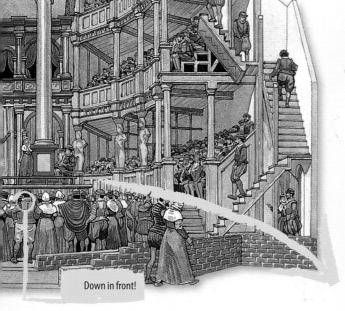

Down in front!

Burning ambition

In 1599, Shakespeare's theater company built its own London playhouse called the Globe. It was only 14 years old when a stage cannon set fire to the roof and the theater burned down. A new Globe was built on this site almost 400 years later.

THIS COSTUME COULD BE A PROBLEM...

Some people think Shakespeare didn't write his own plays.

Bard act to follow

Shakespeare wasn't just a writer, he was a performer, too, working with a leading company in London. Back in those days, actors were expected to perform their own stunts, and young boys played the roles of women.

WANT MORE?

Shakespeare's Globe—www.shakespeares-globe.org

PEEWWW— THE GREAT STINK

Picture this: it's 150 years ago and it's a scorching hot summer. The River Thames is full of rotting food, human waste, and dead animals. There's no clean water, and the smell is so bad it's sending people crazy. Crazier still, they can't work out what's causing the smell!

THIS KITTY IS JUST LITTER.

Toshers
Once the London sewers were built, "toshers" scavenged through them looking for anything of value. This was a job for the whole family.

Flusher men
They flushed out anything stuck in the new sewers.

Nature's solution was simple: rain washed the filth away...eventually.

CAN YOU GIVE ME A HAND...

Mudlarks
Boys and girls as young as six dug around in the filthy mud on the banks of the Thames for coins.

Rat-catcher
Rats spread disease such as plague, so rat-catchers were paid to get rid of them. Some caught rats with their bare hands, others had dogs.

BUSINESS IS BOOMING!!

C'MON MISTER, WE'RE DOING NO HARM, HONEST!

NO FLUSH RUSH

Most Londoners used simple pots as toilets. Even after the invention of the flushing toilet, human waste still ended up in pits that would eventually overflow into the river, which was also where people got their drinking and washing water. Not good in a hot, dry summer.

Sparkling clean?
These days the water in the Thames is much cleaner. Even swans think so. But at low tide there is still trash to be seen.

WANT MORE?

London sewer history—www.historyfiles.co.uk/FeaturesBritain/Modern_London02

CELEBRITY SPOTTING

Madame Tussaud started by making wax death masks of people killed during the French Revolution. She came to London in 1803 and exhibited 30 models. They were a huge hit because they gave people glimpses of celebrities before photography was widespread and long before the invention of television.

Wax facts

Madame Tussauds creates about 50 figures a year, each one taking up to 6 months to finish. The sculptor uses steel and aluminum rods to build a kind of skeleton, which is filled out with newspaper and held with chicken wire.

CUT AND BLOW DRY

Real human hair is used on the figures, not only on top of the head but also for beards, mustaches, and eyebrows, so it needs regular shampooing and styling. In 1996, surprised staff discovered that Adolf Hitler's hair was still growing and needed a trim.

Waxing lyrical

Shakespeare wrote, "Rich gifts wax poor when givers prove unkind." What would he have thought of his waxwork model?

FIND OUT MORE ABOUT ME ON PAGE 46

CHECK OUT

★ A-List Party
★ A Royal Appointment
★ Chamber of Horrors and Screams
★ Sports Zone

The model professional
The figure of one of the world's best footballers, Cristiano Ronaldo, has been dressed in the Portuguese national team uniform. His sitting with Madame Tussauds' sculptors was held at the Real Madrid training ground.

Larger than life
The biggest model ever created is the comic-book hero, Incredible Hulk. His fingers are thicker than a man's arm.

Which is the real Jamie?
The model of celebrity chef Jamie Oliver doesn't cook, but it does have a stomach that rumbles.

SHE'S A REAL HANDFUL!

Green with envy

WANT MORE?

LONDON BURNING

Burning bacon fat can easily catch fire. That's the moral to the story of the London baker who in 1666 put two big bits of bacon in his oven for the morning and then went to bed. The fat dripped onto his straw-covered floor, a flame lit up, and the fire took hold, spreading to neighboring houses. The citizen firefighting service using buckets of water from the river could not dampen the great fire, and most of London was destroyed.

The baker's mistake
By the time the flames died out 6 days later, around 90 churches, 50 trades halls, and 13,000 houses were burned to the ground. Incredibly, only a few people died.

EXCUSE ME!!

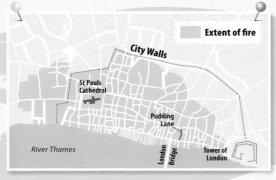

Extent of fire

City Walls

St Pauls Cathedral

Pudding Lane

River Thames

London Bridge

Tower of London

Tour of flames

The fire reached London Bridge but was stopped because part of the bridge had already burned down! It headed down Thames Street where wharves and warehouses caught alight, and spread back into the city.

Tall tribute

A monument to the Great Fire, in the form of a Roman column, stands just a few steps from where the fire first started. It was designed by Sir Christopher Wren.

Nights of terror

Beneath a fiery-red night sky, people ran from their homes and headed to the safety of the river.

WANT MORE?

MILITARY MONKS

A mix of priest and professional soldier, the Templars would go to battle as a heavily armored advance force, or ride into war on horseback as part of the light cavalry. Others took on peaceful support roles as farmers or ministers, looking after a knight's finances while he was away at war.

Poles apart
There were many Knights Templar flags, most of which featured a red cross. But they also had a naval flag with a skull and crossbones on it!

Seal of approval
Seals were like signatures in a time when most people couldn't read or write. The text on the great seal of the Knights Templar reads (in Latin) "The Seal of the Soldiers of Christ."

KNIGHTS IN THE CITY

The Temple Church in London was built in the 12th century as the English headquarters of the Knights Templar. This is where they held their initiation ceremonies.

Set in stone
There are 10 life-sized knight sculptures laid out on the church floor. These were thought to be tombs until it was discovered that there are no bodies under them.

Round the outside
The Temple Church is famous for its unusual shape—one section is round to be like the circular Church of the Holy Sepulchre in Jerusalem.

The first Templar headquarters was in Jerusalem.

Joining up
Knights Templar initiation ceremonies were called "receptions." They were secret affairs, which made some people suspicious of what they were doing.

I HEREBY SAY GOODNIGHT TO THE KNIGHTS!

End of the order
King Philip IV of France threatened Pope Clement with military action if he didn't put an end to the Knights Templar, so the Pope dissolved the order.

WANT MORE?

GROOVY, BABY

After years in a deep freeze, British secret agent Austin Powers is defrosted to save the world. Naturally he is still wearing the clothes of the 1960s, a time when London was on fashion fire with its funky outfits. These days London is famous for Jimmy Choo shoes and Ben Sherman shirts.

DO YOU WANT MINI OR MICRO MINI?

Mary and the mini
A big name in sixties fashion was Mary Quant, who is credited with creating the mini-skirt and the micro-mini, as well as the "wet look" that included shiny vinyl boots called "go-go" boots.

London leads the way
In the 1960s, young people rebelled against the stuffy old world and embraced radical new styles. Carnaby Street was where the coolest people found the hottest fashions.

Bright disposable dresses made of paper were a brief craze in sixties London.

YES, I ADMIT IT, I'M COOL.

Style file
With the popularity of retro and vintage fashion—anything more than 15 years old—London second-hand markets like Camden Road and Portobello Road are treasure troves.

IF THE SHOE FITS...

Two of the best known shoe designers in the world found their feet thanks to recognition from London fashion experts. Both have headquarters in London.

Jimmy Choo
Jimmy Choo hit the big time when Tamara Mellon from *British Vogue* asked Mr. Choo to go into business with her, selling uber-cool shoes.

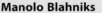

Manolo Blahniks
Manolo Blahnik found fame after hip London designer Ossie Clark used his shoes in a fashion collection.

I'M THE GRAND OLD LADY OF PUNK!

QUEEN OF OUTRAGEOUS

Vivienne Westwood attracted worldwide attention in the 1970s with designs based on the London punk style—ripped T-shirts, chains, heavy makeup, and spiked hair. In the 1980s, as punk died out, she created a whole different look with a pirate twist that became the height of fashion.

Busy buying
Just about every major department store and chain has a shop on Oxford Street, and there are hundreds of boutiques, making it the busiest shopping street in London.

WANT MORE?

Victoria and Albert Museum—www.vam.ac.uk/page/f/fashion

DRAKE AROUND THE WORLD

Not everyone would be thrilled at the prospect of setting off toward an empty horizon, with only muscle and wind power to drive you forward through massive seas. It was a job for the fearless or the foolish, the needy or the greedy. Sir Francis Drake was all of these. Under his command, the English gained wealth and came in contact with new foods and cultures. But he was also a pirate, a slave trader, and a man who would do anything to get what he wanted.

I'VE DISCOVERED THE POTATO!

Astronomical!
GPS was a long way off in the future when Drake sailed around the world! He used an instrument called a mariner's astrolabe to work out where he was and where he should be going.

AROUND THE WORLD

Drake left home at twelve years of age to go to sea, so by the time he was given the orders to take a fleet of English ships around the world for the first time, he knew what he was doing! The expedition took him three years, from 1577 to 1580.

Queen explorer

Queen Elizabeth I, who was in power for most of Drake's life, was an ambitious ruler. She commissioned the expedition to go around the world.

WE SPANIARDS CALL HIM THE DRAGON!

THANKS DRAKE, IT'S MASHING!

MONEY AND MAPS

Drake's trips brought England monetary wealth as well as wealth of knowledge. His attacks on the Spanish fleets scored masses of gold and silver, and his voyages gave mapmakers more to work with as they built a true picture of how the world was laid out.

Old gold

When Drake left to circle the globe, he commanded a fleet of five ships. He was on the ship *Pelican*. Within a year all ships except the *Pelican* were lost. Drake renamed her the *Golden Hinde*.

SO TELL ME AGAIN, HOW DO I GET DOWN?

WANT MORE?

Golden Hinde replica—www.goldenhinde.com

I WANT A TURN IN THE CARRIAGE!

NOW THAT'S WHAT I CALL BIG CITY LIGHTS!

ON WITH THE SHOW

The procession of the Lord Mayor through the streets of London has taken place every year for over 800 years. Despite disasters like the Great Fire, the Plague, and the bombing of London in World War II, the show goes on. These days the main issue is security— around 3,500 manholes have to be searched.

NOTHING TO SEE DOWN HERE I SWEAR!

Boom town
A highlight of the Lord Mayor's Show held every November is the fireworks display over the Thames River that burns through more than a half-ton of explosives!

MEOW!

Statue of Tommy

WHIT AND WHISKERS

You may have read about the former Sheriff and Lord Mayor of London, Sir Richard Whittington, in the children's folktale *Dick Whittington and His Cat*. He starts out as a poor boy and makes his fortune after a series of adventures with his feline friend Tommy.

Guarded by giants

The Lord Mayor is escorted in the procession by huge creatures called Gog and Magog. These mythical protectors of London were once made of wood, but the latest versions are made by basketmakers and are about 65ft (20m) tall.

JUST DRUMMING UP SOME INTEREST IN MY MUSIC.

Musical march

The procession goes for about 3 miles (5km) and includes the bands of the Grenadier Guards, Royal Air Force, and Royal Marines.

WANT MORE?

Lord Mayor's Show official website—www.lordmayorsshow.org

JACK THE RIPPER

Dare you venture into the dark parts of old London? For eight weeks in 1888, the narrow alleys of Whitechapel were a murder scene. Five young women were brutally killed by a murderer called Jack the Ripper. He was never caught.

ANNIE CHAPMAN
HANBURY STREET

FINISH 5

Old Spitalfields Market

SPITALFIELDS

Christ Church, Spitalfields

4

Sandy's Row Synagogue

Mary Jane Kelly
formerly Dorset Street

Street Station

ROADGATE

Liverpool Street

St. Botolph-without-Bishopsgate

BISHOPSGATE

COMMERCIAL STREET

Petticoat Lane Market

MIDDLESEX STREET

Aldgate East

One good thing
The murders led to more police and better houses and street lights for the people in London's East End.

HOUNDSDITCH

DUKE'S PLACE

WHITECHAPEL

ST. BOTOLPH STREET

Aldgate

WHITECHAPEL HIGH ST

YOO-HOO!

YIKES!!

CATHERINE EDDOWES
MITRE SQUARE

3

St Botolph

ALDGATE HIGH STREET

BRAHAM S

N
W E
S

St. Katherine Cree

Aldgate Pump

ALDGATE

Fenchurch Street Station

MAP KEY

† CHURCH		☪ MOSQUE	
H HOSPITAL		✡ SYNAGOGUE	
🚇 LONDON UNDERGROUND STATION		★ LANDMARK OR PLACE OF INTEREST	
🚆 NATIONAL RAIL STATION			

0 metres   50   100   150   200   250
0 yards   50   100   150   200   250

St. Anne's
Catholic Church

I'M THE MAN

MARY ANN NICHOLS
DURWARD STREET
(formerly Buck's Row)

1 START

HE'S NOT
IN HERE

Who was Jack the Ripper?
No one knows! One suspect
was the son of the future
King. Another, a surgeon.

Whitechapel

H

Royal London
Hospital

WHITECHAPEL ROAD

East London
Mosque

ST WAY

Track him down
Despite huge public interest and
a big police investigation, the
murderer was never found.

Royal

IT'S NOT WHITE
ANYMORE...

St. Boniface

Whitechapel
Gallery

COMMERCIAL ROAD

CANNON STR

LEMAN STREET

2 **ELIZABETH STRIDE**
HENRIQUES STREET
(formerly Berner Street)

Whitechapel alleys
The streets and alleys of
Whitechapel were dark and scary
with narrow doorways to hide in.

WANT
MORE?

Jack the Ripper 1888—www.jack-the-ripper.org

Medieval version
The London Bridge with buildings on top lasted over 600 years. Its narrow arches produced dangerous rapids that drowned many foolhardy boatmen.

LONDON BRIDGE NOT FALLING DOWN

The first few London Bridges fell down, burned down, or were hacked down by invaders. This was a problem since it was the only way to cross the River Thames. In the 13th century they built a London Bridge in stone with shops and houses seven stories high. As a special treat, the heads of traitors were stuck on spikes over the bridge and left to rot.

YOU SHOULD QUIT WHILE YOU'RE A HEAD!

c. 1900

Today

Bridge between old and new
The "new" London Bridge—replacing the medieval bridge—opened in 1831. But it was fast outdated, and in 1968 it was sold and shipped to the USA.

These days...
The current London Bridge was opened by the Queen in 1973. It was hit by a British warship, HMS *Jupiter*, in 1984, but it was fully repaired and continues to hold up against ever-increasing amounts of traffic.

LONDON BRIDGE IN ARIZONA

Robert P. McCulloch was a wealthy American who bought London Bridge and had it shipped in pieces to Lake Havasu in Arizona. McCulloch had made his name and his money as an inventor, manufacturer, and property developer. He built Lake Havasu City and bought London Bridge to give the city a special talking point!

WANT MORE?

The London Bridge Museum—www.oldlondonbridge.com

COULD YOU LIVE HERE?

These cosy castles belong to the Queen. Windsor Castle, where the Queen hangs out on weekends, has a thousand rooms, a few dungeons, and a yard that could fit eight football fields. Her home in London, Buckingham Palace, is small by comparison. It only has 775 rooms.

Palace in wonderland
When royal family members are in London they stay at Buckingham Palace, which is also their head office and the place where they hold official events like balls and banquets.

The Royal Standard

HOME SWEET HOME

Windsor Castle has been around for more than 900 years, and is the oldest and largest occupied castle in the world. A great fire in 1992 destroyed more than 100 of its rooms, and it took the next five years to restore them.

It's a small world
Built in the early 1920s, Queen Mary's Dolls' House is not your average toy home. It has electricity, running water, and even a miniature library.

The inside story
The White Drawing Room in Buckingham Palace is famous for its over-the-top ceiling and don't-touch-those decorations. You might recognize the room from royal family photos.

I DON'T KNOW WHERE TO START...

HE'S DRIVING ME BATTY!

DO I LOOK AS SILLY AS HIM IN THIS HAT?

On the march
Soldiers in the Queen's five regiments of foot guards can't stay alert forever, so there is a regular "changing of the guard." Their tall hats are made from the fur of Canadian black bears.

Flying visit
A protester dressed as Batman once climbed up the front wall of Buckingham Palace and almost made it to the balcony where the royal family appears on special occasions.

WANT MORE?

Buckingham Palace has 1,514 doors ✶ The British Monarchy—www.royal.gov.uk

The Square Mile

Silent streets
While the Square Mile is packed with people on weekdays, not many people live in the area, so it becomes a ghost town on weekends.

Old and new
Nowadays there are more skyscrapers than old buildings in the Square Mile, but history stands proud in the Bank of England, the Old Bailey, and St. Paul's Cathedral.

THE HAVES AND

THERE'S NO BETTER WAY TO BEAT THE LONDON TRAFFIC!

The mega-rich of London work and play in a square mile that used to be the original city of London, when it was under Roman rule. The "Square Mile"—still called the City of London—is where billionaires and banks do business. The best bankers and traders get paid millions of pounds each year. And—if they've been good—they might get another million pounds at Christmas as a "bonus." That should buy some nice presents!

Underground scene

Bank Tube station is over 100 years old and is named after the Bank of England. It's been used for disaster-training exercises for the city's emergency services.

IT'S GOOD TO BE ME!

HAVE YACHTS

The Square Mile is on the site of ancient Londinium.

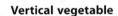

Making a quid

The headquarters of the Bank of England has been located in the Square Mile for almost 300 years. It is the government's central bank, which issues all the banknotes in England.

Vertical vegetable

The unusual 30 St. Mary Axe skyscraper is known as the "Gherkin." During construction the grave of a Roman girl was discovered. It was removed, then returned to the base of the completed building.

£5
£20
£10

WANT MORE?

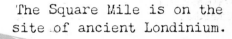

ON THE ROAD

One of the many myths about London cabbies is that even though their taxis are motorized, the law still says they must carry a bale of hay and a sack of oats, and that the council has to supply a water trough at the taxi rank. Not true. It wasn't true even when cabs were horse-drawn!

The scoop on travel
The first buses were omnibuses. Omnibus means "for everyone." They could take more people than the smaller hackney carriages—but they also put more manure on the streets!

Bus in 1950   *Bus in 1948*   *Bus today*

BUS HISTORY

The famous red Routemaster London buses started cruising the streets in 1956 and kept services running until 2005, though more modern buses were introduced in the meantime. Now a new Routemaster bus is being designed using fuel-efficient, environmentally friendly equipment and technology.

Catch me if you can
The old London buses didn't have doors. If you could run fast enough, you could jump on board between stops.

Serious knowledge
To drive a cab in all parts of London you must pass "the knowledge"—a test of 320 routes plus major places of interest. No wonder it can take four years to get a license!

IS THIS GUY INSANE?

Bye bye bus conductors
When the Routemaster was retired, it was the end of the road for conductors. Modern buses don't need two people, so Londoners farewelled their sometimes quirky conductors.

OF COURSE I WAS SAD TO GO, BUT YOU CAN'T STOP PROGRESS...

WANT MORE?

London Transport Museum—www.ltmuseum.co.uk

TOWER OF TORTURE

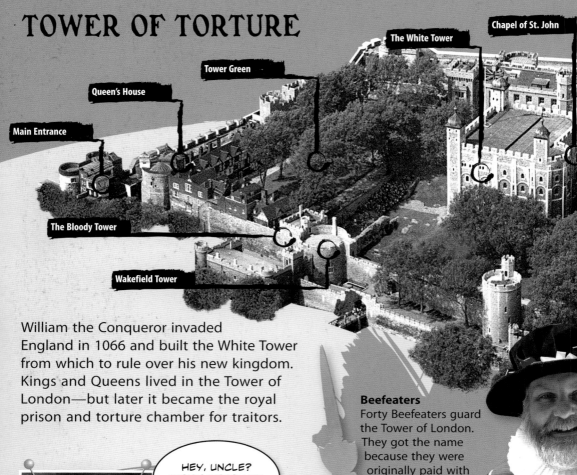

Chapel of St. John

The White Tower

Tower Green

Queen's House

Main Entrance

The Bloody Tower

Wakefield Tower

William the Conqueror invaded England in 1066 and built the White Tower from which to rule over his new kingdom. Kings and Queens lived in the Tower of London—but later it became the royal prison and torture chamber for traitors.

Beefeaters
Forty Beefeaters guard the Tower of London. They got the name because they were originally paid with beef instead of money.

> HEY, UNCLE? WE'RE READY TO GO HOME NOW.

LOST PRINCES

The two young sons of King Edward IV were locked up in the Tower by their evil uncle Richard so that he could become king. They were last seen there in 1483. In 1674 two boys' skeletons were found under a staircase in the Tower. Suspicious?

The last beheading here was in 1747.

GREAT STUFF

THESE PEOPLE ARE DRIVING ME RAVEN MAD.

Black birds
Seven ravens live in the Tower. Legend says England will fall if they ever leave.

Hands off!
The Crown Jewels are kept in a strongroom and guarded by soldiers.

Royal scepter

The lesson is always be nice to the King!

I WANT HIM FLAT AS A PANCAKE.

Stretch the truth
Until 1640, people were stretched on the "rack" to make them confess to crimes against the King.

WANT MORE?

Tower of London—www.hrp.org.uk/toweroflondon

BACKYARD BLITZ

Every night for 76 nights during World War II London was bombed by German aircraft. It was known as the Blitz—Blitz is short for the German word "Blitzkrieg," which means lightning war. The warning whoop of the air-raid sirens and the pitch dark of the blackouts became part of daily life.

YOU SAID IT!

WHAT A MESS!

Railway sleepers
When German aircraft started dropping bombs on London after dark, many people decided it was safer to sleep in the city's underground train stations than at home.

It's a miracle!
Even though St. Paul's Cathedral sits on top of the highest hill in the city, it made it through the Blitz with only a little damage.

> I'M SURE THERE WAS A HOUSE HERE BEFORE...

RELIVING HISTORY

The only reminders Londoners want of the war are those in the museums. The Imperial War Museum has displays that show what London was like during wartime. Part of the museum is on the HMS *Belfast*, a real World War II battle cruiser floating on the River Thames.

Above: Imperial War Museum
Left: Churchill Museum and Cabinet War Room

Shelter from harm

Underground air-raid shelters were provided free to most Londoners. You buried a steel Anderson shelter behind your house and hopped in it when the bombing started.

We are not amused!

Buckingham Palace was bombed seven times in the Blitz. Once the palace chapel was completely destroyed, but King George VI and Queen Elizabeth were never harmed.

WANT MORE?

King-sized sturgeon
In 1947 this super-sized sturgeon was caught in the English Channel and offered to the king before being sold to a London store. The fish weighed 400lb (180kg) —just a little heavier than you?

ONE MUST HAVE PERMISSION BEFORE ONE EATS ME.

ANIMAL KINGDOM

The royals rule not only over the people of the United Kingdom, but also over some of the creatures as well. By law, sturgeons, whales, dolphins, or porpoises caught in British waters belong to the current king or queen. Royal permission must be given before the animal can be kept, eaten, given away, or sold. The law was brought in to stop over-fishing, because these animals were either good to eat or useful for their bones, like whalebone, which was used in women's clothing.

Swanning about
The wild swans that live on the River Thames are part-owned by the kings and queens of England. Every year the swans are counted and given a royal health check. The tradition, which started over 800 years ago, is called swan "upping."

Say neigh

Royals and horses go hand in hand, literally. The Queen, her kids, and her grandkids are all into polo, show jumping, and cross-country. The Queen is also keen on breeding and training horses.

A dog's tale

Corgis have been the Queen's favorite since her dad, King George VI, gave her a corgi from a local kennel. The dog's name was Dookie. Since then she's owned many corgis and even mated them with dachshunds to create dorgis!

HEATHER
BORN MAY 28. 1961
DIED JAN. 31. 1977
FOR 15 YEARS THE
FAITHFUL COMPANION
OF THE QUEEN.
GREAT GRAND
DAUGHTER OF SUSAN

Doggie demise

The royal corgi Heather died aged 15 and was buried at Sandringham House, which is the private residence used by the Queen in winter.

Some royal pets have their own portraits!

I'M TOLD I WAS HARD TO WRAP.

ANIMAL GIFTS

The Queen is sometimes given live gifts! She's had a canary from Germany, jaguars and sloths from Brazil, two black beavers from Canada, two giant turtles from the Seychelles, and an elephant from Cameroon.

TWEET!

WANT MORE?

Royal animals—www.royal.gov.uk/TheRoyalHousehold/RoyalAnimals/Overview.aspx

CHOP OFF HIS HEAD!

Having your head chopped off was the least painful punishment for crimes against the Crown and Church, and you had to be pretty posh to be executed this way. Everyone else was hanged, burned at the stake, boiled in oil, or hung, drawn, and quartered, which meant having your guts pulled out, your head chopped off, and your body cut into four pieces!

Field of fear
There was no better place to witness public executions, revolts, and assassinations than Smithfield. Executions were carried out here for about 500 years.

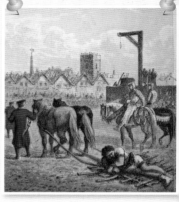

Heading down the river
The water-gate entry to the Tower of London is called Traitors' Gate because that's where prisoners charged with treason were taken inside. On the way, they passed the heads of executed prisoners displayed on London Bridge.

Most beheadings were carried out at Tower Hill near the Tower of London.

WELL AT LEAST WE GET A GOOD VIEW!

PEOPLE TREAT ME LIKE A NOBODY!

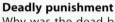

THE PERSONAL TOUCH

You had to be really special to be beheaded in private, like a baron, an earl, or the wife of a king. Such executions were carried out on the Tower Green in the Tower of London (see pages 72–73).

> MY HEAD WAS DISPLAYED FOR 24 YEARS!

Henry VIII had two wives beheaded on the Tower Green.

Tower of terror
More than 100 people have been hanged, beheaded, or shot at the Tower of London over the centuries. The Tower was the prison, while the executions were mostly carried out on Tower Hill.

Deadly punishment
Why was the dead body of Oliver Cromwell dug up and hung, drawn, and quartered? Because Cromwell had ordered the execution of Charles I, and Charles II was still really angry about it.

Bad career choice
The second Earl of Essex, Robert Devereux, was beheaded for following a disastrous military campaign in Ireland with an attempted rebellion against Queen Elizabeth I.

A spot of reign
Lady Jane Grey was only seventeen when she became Queen of England in 1553...and was the same age when she lost the throne nine days later! She was executed the following year.

↓ *The Execution of Lady Jane Grey, 1833, Hippolyte (Paul) Delaroche*

WANT MORE?

Tower of London—www.hrp.org.uk/toweroflondon

HENRY THE COPPER-NOSE KING

When the money left to him by his father ran out, Henry VIII had the Royal Mint make more. However, the silver dip they used was poor quality and it quickly wore away from the etching of his nose. Underneath was the copper base, which is how he got his nickname.

Henry VIII coins

The big time
King Henry added the Great Hall to Hampton Court Palace and lined it with tapestries woven with gold and silver threads.

Money couldn't buy him love
Henry VIII had six wives over a period of 38 years! They were all distant relatives of the King.

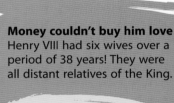

2 Anne Boleyn Beheaded!

3 Jane Seymour Died

I Catherine of Aragon Marriage annulled

A-MAZING!

Hedge your bets
Hampton Court's famous maze wasn't around in Henry VIII's time, but it might have replaced one that he had built for his friend, Cardinal Wolsey.

Spare no expense!
This over-the-top ceiling installed by the King in the Chapel Royal has been cleaned and retouched to make it glitter as it did in his day.

HAIR TODAY, GONE TOMORROW

A 460-year-old lock of hair possibly taken from the head of Henry VIII's last wife, Catherine Parr, was sold in 2008 to a man who lives in one of Catherine's old homes. It cost him £2,160.

4 Anne of Cleves
Marriage annulled

5 Catherine Howard
Beheaded!

6 Catherine Parr
Outlived Henry

WANT MORE?

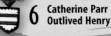

£100

THE A... ISLIN...

£200

PAY £200

£60

WHITECHAPEL ROAD

£60

OLD KENT ROAD

£200 SA... AS YOU PASS

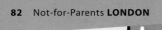

King's Cross Station
London's east coast main line terminus is also home to platform 9¾ in *Harry Potter*.

King's Cross

> BUT WHY IS THE KING SO CROSS?

ROLL THE DICE...

So many people grow up learning about London from the board game Monopoly! The game was invented in the United States by Elizabeth Magie. She called it "The Landlord's Game" because it showed how unfair and unbalanced the world can become when one person owns all the property. The name was changed to Monopoly, meaning total control by one person or company.

Mayfair
As it is in real life, this is the most expensive property you can buy in the game. It's actually an area, not a street, and is named after a fair that was held every year near Hyde Park Corner.

LIV...

...ER ...X

> NO, YOU CAN'T USE A MONOPOLY CARD TO GET OUT OF JAIL.

£400   PAY £100   £350

QUIZ

1. WHAT TRAIN STATION ON THE MONOPOLY BOARD IS FEATURED IN THE *HARRY POTTER* BOOKS?

2. WHAT WAS MONOPOLY ORIGINALLY CALLED?

3. IS PENTONVILLE JAIL ON PENTONVILLE ROAD?

4. WHAT EVENT IS MAYFAIR NAMED AFTER?

5. WHAT WILL YOU FIND A LOT OF IN LEICESTER SQUARE?

Answers: 1. King's Cross; 2. The Landlord's Game; 3. No!; 4. A fair; 5. Cinemas

Leicester Square

This area is in the heart of London's famous West End theater district, and the square is all about cinema.

Bond Street

This schmancy shopping strip is actually two streets in one—the smaller southern section is Old Bond Street and the rest is New Bond Street. It's in the Mayfair area.

Go directly to jail

On your way to jail, don't get lost. Pentonville Prison is actually in Caledonian Road, not Pentonville Road.

WANT MORE?

REMEMBER, REMEMBER

The plot is uncovered
Fawkes and 12 friends spent the year of 1605 plotting how to kill King James and other nobles. They thought it was the only way to stop the persecution of Catholics in England. Sadly for Fawkes, though happily for the King, a tip-off foiled plans. Fawkes was captured before he could light the gunpowder.

Fawkes's confession was signed "Guido," the name he'd used as a soldier in Spain.

By the light of a lantern
Fawkes first tried to dig a tunnel under Parliament but that was too hard, so he rented a room in the basement. He had just one lantern to light his way in the pitch-black.

THE FIFTH OF NOVEMBER

Guy Fawkes was feeling confident. For months he had been sneaking barrels of gunpowder into a storeroom below Parliament, ready for the day when he would blow the place up. On November 5 he had all 36 barrels ready to go. He just had to wait for the King and his Lords to be seated before he would light a match and blow the place sky high...

SORRY KING JAMES, IT'S NOTHING PERSONAL....

Long live the King
The night Guy Fawkes was captured, bonfires were lit in London to celebrate the King's safety. Each year since, on November 5, bonfires and fireworks light the skies.

BIGGEST BONFIRE
Call it Bonfire Night, Guy Fawkes Night, or Guy Fawkes Day, one of the biggest bonfires happens in the town of Lewes, not far from London. In Lewes on November 5 they not only remember Guy Fawkes and the gunpowder plot, but also Protestants burned at the stake by Catholics.

WANT MORE?

Fawkes broke his neck before he was executed. ☆ Parliament—www.parliament.uk

TOP OF THE POPS

From music megastars to one-hit wonders, London has been a birthplace of hip music and pop culture style for over 50 years. Every era, from Glitter Rock to Britpop, had its defining sound and inspired the next generation of young musicians, not only in England but also throughout the world.

00s

90s

80s

1980s music
The hard-core lyrics and violent fashion of punk soon gave way to the electronic sounds of "new wave" music from bands like The Pet Shop Boys and "new romantic" pop rock from Duran Duran, Spandau Ballet, and Culture Club.

70s

60s

1960s music
The fifties kick-started music that had parents the world over covering their ears and eyes. But they hadn't seen anything yet. London in the sixties really got the musical revolution going with rival groups The Rolling Stones and The Beatles sending chills through teenage spines!

Queen

1970s music
This was the era of big stadium shows with outrageous costumes and flamboyant makeup. The biggest stars of the seventies included solo artists Elton John and David Bowie and the band Queen.

The Rolling Stones

The Beatles

Elton John

2000s music

Solo singer-songwriter female artists from London hit the global stage with the "tell it like it is" lyrics of Lily Allen and the X-factor of Leona Lewis.

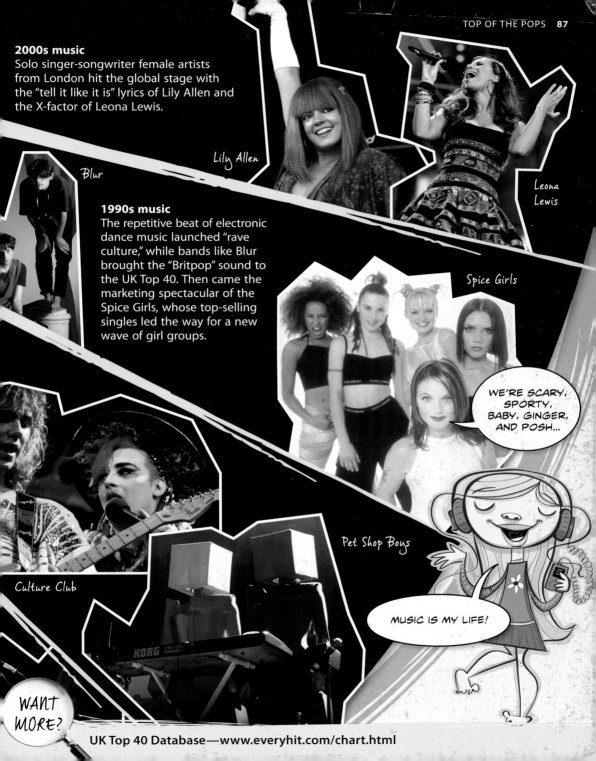

Blur

Lily Allen

Leona Lewis

1990s music

The repetitive beat of electronic dance music launched "rave culture," while bands like Blur brought the "Britpop" sound to the UK Top 40. Then came the marketing spectacular of the Spice Girls, whose top-selling singles led the way for a new wave of girl groups.

Spice Girls

WE'RE SCARY, SPORTY, BABY, GINGER, AND POSH...

Pet Shop Boys

Culture Club

MUSIC IS MY LIFE!

WANT MORE?

UK Top 40 Database—www.everyhit.com/chart.html

HAVING A BALL

There's really only one sport in London, and that's football (don't call it soccer!). There are five clubs that play regularly in the Premier League, plus many others in lower divisions. They all have fanatical followers and local rivalries stretching back to the 19th century—so be careful where you wear your favorite team's uniform, which is known as a "strip."

BET YOU CAN'T BEND IT LIKE ME.

End of the road
In the past, kids could be found kicking a ball around in nearly every street in London. Now the amount of traffic on the roads makes this a rare sight.

Becks!
Football superstar David Beckham was born in East London, but his parents were Manchester United fans. So it was no surprise when he joined Manchester, even though as a boy he played for Tottenham.

PERFECT PITCH

Football is the most popular sport in London, but there are plenty of fanatical rugby fans as well. In summer, attention turns to the Wimbledon tennis tournament. And if tennis isn't your thing, there's always cricket.

TOP TEAMS

There are five topflight football teams in London—two from the north of the city and two from the west—plus one from the East End called West Ham!

OFF THE ROAD—THERE'S A CAR COMING!

LUCKY FOR YOU, 'COS ONLY A CAR CAN STOP ME!

ARSENAL TILL I DIE!

No love lost

The greatest rivalry in London football is between Arsenal and Tottenham fans, who more than anything want their team to beat the other in the North London derby.

WANT MORE?

1 Arsenal F.C.

Perhaps the most famous club in London, Arsenal is definitely the most successful. Players wear red and white at their home ground, which is Emirates Stadium.

2 Chelsea F.C.

Chelsea has recently become a big club financed by a Russian billionaire. Players wear blue and white at their home ground, Stamford Bridge.

3 Fulham F.C.

London's oldest professional football team has never won a major trophy. Players wear white and black at their home ground, Craven Cottage.

4 Tottenham F.C.

Arsenal's neighbors have won a major trophy in each of the last six decades. Players wear white and navy-blue at their home ground, White Hart Lane.

5 West Ham F.C.

First known as Thames Ironworks F.C., West Ham has been around for more than 110 years. Players wear claret and sky-blue at their home ground, Upton Park.

The English Football Association—www.thefa.com

AN ARTFUL LESSON

William Hogarth was part artist, part cartoonist. His work was often a comment on political events and on human nature. He started as a printer, creating book illustrations, posters, and pamphlets, and then turned to painting. Some of his best-known works are his "morality paintings" which show humans in tragic party mode.

GIN IS THE DEVIL'S DRINK! [EVIL LAUGH]

↓ *Gin Lane*
1751, William Hogarth

Sinful gin

Hogarth watched as London became crazed with alcohol, especially gin, after the government made it cheap to buy. His 1751 etching *Gin Lane* showed the effects the "Gin Craze" was having on families and became the pin-up image for the campaign against cheap gin.

CAN YOU FIND...

A BUILDING COLLAPSING

A TRADESMAN SELLING HIS TOOLS TO A PAWNBROKER

A SHOP SELLING GIN

A MAN SHARING A BONE WITH A DOG

A MOTHER FEEDING GIN TO HER BABY

↓ *Beer Street*
  1751, William Hogarth

BE AN ANGEL, AND
GET ME A BEER?

CAN YOU FIND...

BUILDERS AT WORK

A MAN PAINTING A PUB SIGN

A PAWNBROKER'S BUSINESS
GONE TO RUIN

A HUGE LEG OF HAM

TWO BASKETS FULL OF FISH

Brilliant beer

Hogarth's *Beer Street* was like the flip side to *Gin Lane*. Beer at the time was considered calming and healthy. Unlike the violent scenes in *Gin Lane*, the people in *Beer Street* are cheerful, healthy, and industrious.

STIFF COMPETITION

In some poor districts of London during the "Gin Craze" one in every four houses was also a gin shop. Beer brewers competed by starting up more alehouses, so London by the late 1700s was like one big pub! Nowadays there are about 3,800 pubs in London, and it is against the law to serve customers who are drunk.

WANT
MORE?

Hogarth's House Museum—www.hounslow.info/arts/hogarthshouse

WHAT'S IN A NAME?

Many of the streets in London are named after the trade, job, or activity that took place in the street at the time. Try the quiz to see if you can guess which action matches the street name.

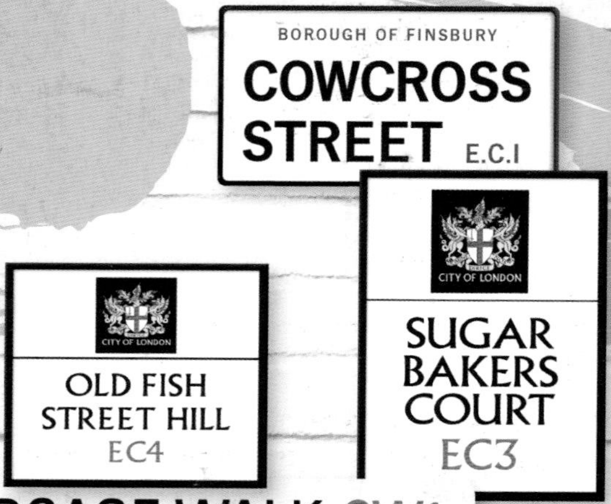

BOROUGH OF FINSBURY

COWCROSS STREET E.C.1

SUGAR BAKERS COURT EC3

OLD FISH STREET HILL EC4

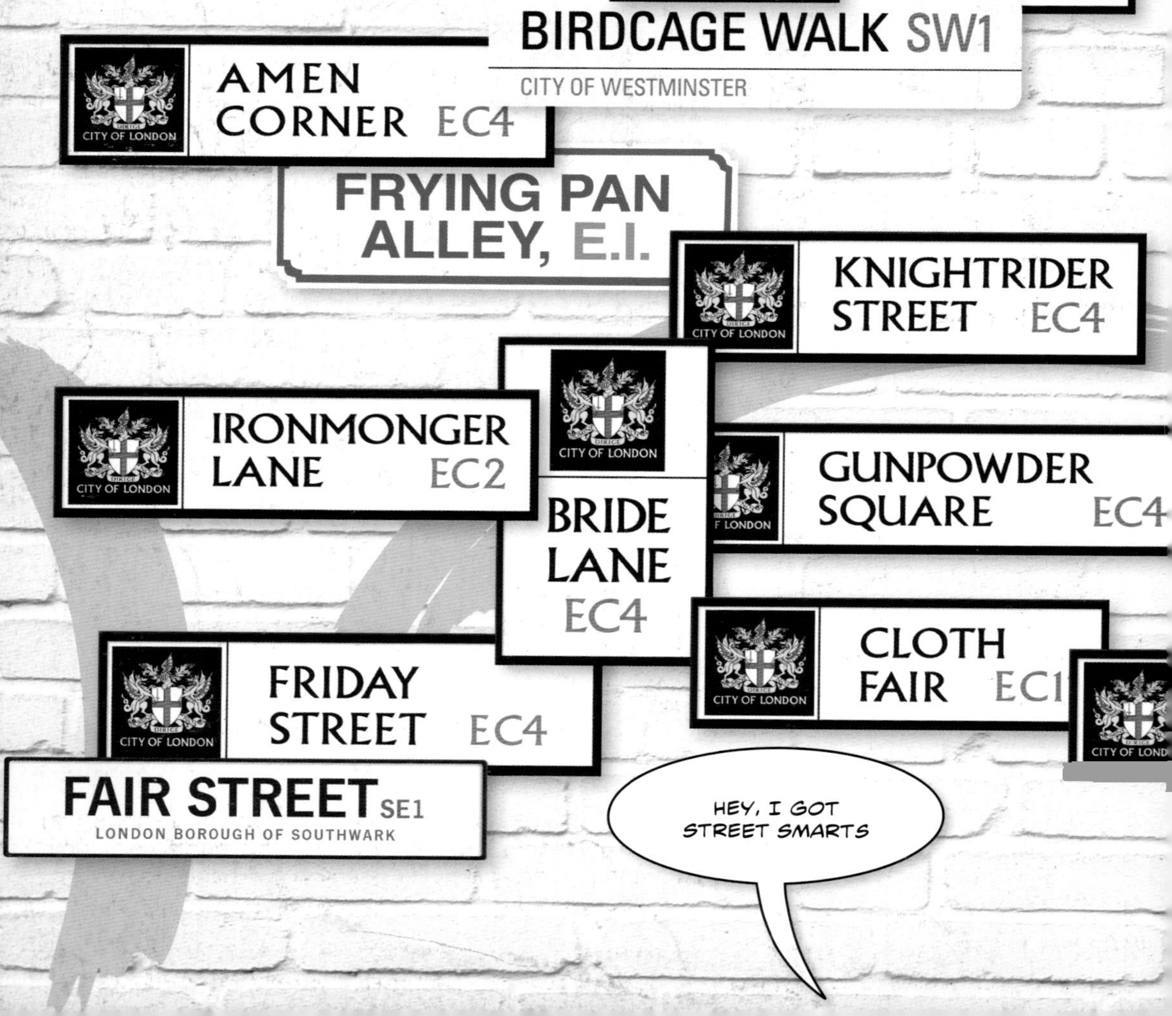

BIRDCAGE WALK SW1
CITY OF WESTMINSTER

AMEN CORNER EC4

FRYING PAN ALLEY, E.I.

KNIGHTRIDER STREET EC4

IRONMONGER LANE EC2

BRIDE LANE EC4

GUNPOWDER SQUARE EC4

CLOTH FAIR EC1

CITY OF LONDON

FRIDAY STREET EC4

FAIR STREET SE1
LONDON BOROUGH OF SOUTHWARK

HEY, I GOT STREET SMARTS

HANGING SWORD ALLEY EC4

LOVE LANE EC2

CITY OF LONDON I-39 THREADNEEDLE STREET E.C.2.

TURNAGAIN LANE EC4

PUDDING LANE EC3

SHOE LANE EC4

CHEAPSIDE EC2

HROGMORTON REET EC2

STREET QUIZ

1. The corner next to a cathedral where people said their prayers.
2. Where Charles II kept exotic birds in a cage (including a crane with a wooden leg).
3. Where a market called a "chepe" was held.
4. This is where England's biggest cloth fair was held at the time of Elizabeth I.
5. Cattle had to cross here on their way to the slaughterhouse.
6. The site of the once famous Horsleydown Fair.
7. Street of the fishmongers who went to market on Fridays.
8. The place to go to buy tools and hardware.
9. Knights rode down this street from the Tower of London.
10. Lane in London where people in love liked to go for a walk.
11. Named for a shoe-shaped piece of land.
12. The home of Sir Nicholas Throgmorton, an ambassador to France.
13. This lane is a dead end so you have to turn again at the end.

1. Amen Corner; 2. Birdcage Walk; 3. Cheapside; 4. Cloth Fair; 5. Cowcross Street; 6. Fair Street; 7. Friday Street; 8. Ironmonger Lane; 9. Knightrider Street; 10. Love Lane; 11. Shoe Lane; 12. Throgmorton Street; 13. Turnagain Lane

WANT MORE?

Origins of London Street Names—www.londononline.co.uk/streetorigins

INDEX

NOT-FOR-PARENTS
LONDON
EVERYTHING YOU EVER WANTED TO KNOW

1st Edition
Published August 2011

Conceived by Weldon Owen in partnership with Lonely Planet
Produced by Weldon Owen Pty Ltd
Weldon Owen Pty Ltd
59–61 Victoria Street, McMahons Point
Sydney NSW 2060, Australia

Copyright © 2011 Weldon Owen Pty Ltd

WELDON OWEN PTY LTD
Managing Director Kay Scarlett
Publisher Corinne Roberts
Creative Director Sue Burk
Senior Vice President,
International Sales Stuart Laurence
Sales Manager, North America Ellen Towell
Administration Manager,
International Sales Kristine Ravn
Managing Editor Averil Moffat
Project Editor Lachlan McLaine
Designer Agnieszka Rozycka
Images Manager Trucie Henderson
Production Director Todd Rechner
Production and Prepress Controller Mike Crowton

Published by
Lonely Planet Publications Pty Ltd ABN 36 005 607 983
90 Maribyrnong St, Footscray, Victoria 3011, Australia

ISBN 978-1-74220-816-9

Printed in Singapore

A WELDON OWEN PRODUCTION

Credits and acknowledgments

Key tcl=top center left; tl=top left; tc=top center; tcr=top center right; tr=top right; cl=center left; c=center; cr=center right; bcl=bottom center left; bl=bottom left; bc=bottom center; bcr=bottom center right; br=bottom right; bg=background

20cl, 22tr, 24c, 25br, 27cl, tr, 28c, 32cr, 35bcr, bc; 43br, 44bc, cr, 45cl, 56bl, tr, 64-65bc, 68br, 70tr, tcl, cl, tc, 71cr, 79tr, 82cl, 82-83bg, 86bc, 86-87t, 87bc, 88-89tc **Alamy**; 19tc, 64tc, 79br **Bridgeman Art Library**; 10cl, 10-11c, 11cl, tl, 12cl, 13tcl, cr, bcl, 15bl, br, 20-21tr, 29tc, 30tc, c, 33c, 34-35tl, 36bl, bc, 37bcr, 42-43c, 43bl, 45cr, 49tr, 50br, bcl, tcl, 50-51bc, 51tc, cr, 55cr, bl, 57tc, 60cr, 60-61tl, 61tl, c, 66c, 67bc, 72-73tc, 73cl, cr, c; 74cr, 75tr, 76tl, 77c, 80bl, 83bc, 86c, 87cr, tc **Corbis**; 38bc **DigitalStock**; 9bl, 11bc, 16cr, 17bc, tl, tr, cr, 18tr, 18-19c, 19c, 23cl, br, 30bc, 31br, 33cl, 35tc, 36cr, 37tc, cl, 38-39tc, 38cl, 40c, 44cl, 45c, 47tr, 53cr, 54bc, 57cr, br, 61tr, 65cr, cl, 66cr, bl, 67cr, 74bc, 74-75cl, 75cl, br, 76tr, br, 77tl, 80tr, 81cr, 82br, 84cl, br, 86bl, 86-87bc, c, tc, 88cl, 88-89bc **Getty Images**; 8br, bl, 9c, br, tr, 14cl, bc, 15tc, 16cl, 17c, 18cl, 18-19br, 20bl, bc, 21cr, 23tr, 25tl, 27cl, 28tl, 30br, 32br, 37tl, 38c, 39cr, 40tl, 40-41c, 41br, 42cl, 43cl, 44bl, c, 45tl, 46cl, tl, 46-47bg, 49br, 50bl, 53br, 54cr, 55br, 56tl, 57tl, 60bc, 61bc, 64c, 67cl, 68tl, 69bl, 73tr, 76cr, tl, 78c, 80tr, 84-85b, 85tl, 87br, 88bc, 89tcr, br, c, bcr, bc, 92-93bg **iStockphoto.com**; 28-29bg, 39tc, 68-69c, 82c **Lonely Planet**; 4cr, 8tc, 9cl, 11br, 14cr, 15c, 20br, 24-25bc, 25tr, 26-27bg, 32cl, 33tc, bl, cr, br, 35tcr, 36c, tr, 37bl, cr, 40-41tr, 43tr, 44tr, 45cr, 50tr, 53bl, 55tc, 56-57c, 61c, 65c, 66cl, 69tl, 70tr, 72-73bc, 75c, 78cr, 79c, 80bc, br, cl, 81cl, br, tc, tl, bc, 82tl, 83cr, 85cr, br, cl, **Photolibrary**; 31bcr, bcl, bl, c, tc, tcr **Photoshot**; 29cr **Richard Seaman**; 66-67tr **The Royal Collection**; 9cr, 12cr, 13tr, 18bl, 21cl, br, 22c, cr, 23c, 31bg, 35cl, 40bc, 47br **Shutterstock**; 25c, 39bc, **Superstock**; 1tr, bc, tc, 4-5bg, 20tr, 76c, 82tr, 86-87bg **VectorStock**; 18-19bc, 21bl, 23bl, 31c, 72bl, 79tl, 80tc, 89tcr, cr, bcr, c, br **Wikipedia**

All repeated image motifs courtesy of **iStockphoto.com**.

Illustrations
Cover illustrations by Chris Corr

30bl, 54l, 70tr, 72-73, 78br, 84tr **Faz Choudhury/The Art Agency**; 44c, 60-61c **Francesca D'Ottavi/Wilkinson Studios**; 66-67tc, 72, 90tr **Dave Smith/The Art Agency**

Maps 36, 46, 54 Peter Bull Art Studio

All illustrations and maps copyright 2011 Weldon Owen Pty Ltd.

LONELY PLANET OFFICES

Australia Head Office
Locked Bag 1, Footscray, Victoria 3011
Phone 03 8379 8000 Fax 03 8379 8111
Email talk2us@lonelyplanet.com.au

USA
150 Linden St, Oakland, CA 94607
Phone 510 250 6400 Toll free 800 275 8555 Fax 510 893 8572
Email info@lonelyplanet.com

UK
2nd fl, 186 City Rd, London EC1V 2NT
Phone 020 7106 2100 Fax 020 7106 2101
Email go@lonelyplanet.co.uk